UPDATED EDITION

101 CELLO TI[...]

STUFF ALL THE PROS KNOW [...]

T0068348

BY ANGELA SCHMIDT

Recording Credits
Recorded at BeatHouse Music, Milwaukee, WI
Jim Reith, Engineer

To access audio visit:
www.halleonard.com/mylibrary

Enter Code
1799-9847-5277-3670

ISBN 978-1-4950-3084-0

7777 W. BLUEMOUND RD. P.O. BOX 13819 MILWAUKEE, WI 53213

In Australia Contact:
Hal Leonard Australia Pty. Ltd.
4 Lentara Court
Cheltenham, Victoria, 3192 Australia
Email: ausadmin@halleonard.com.au

Visit Hal Leonard Online at
www.halleonard.com

TABLE OF CONTENTS

1 THE CELLO AND BOW
(HANDLE WITH CARE)

The cello body is large and hollow, and is almost always made of wood (spruce and maple). The top (or front) and bottom panels are slightly curved. The fingerboard, tailpiece, and pegs are usually made of ebony. Be very careful when handling the cello, especially around the bridge, for it is not glued in place, and can break or fall. Do not turn the cello pegs until you know how to tune the cello. If you need to carry the cello, grasp it firmly around the neck, and carry it so you can see the bridge and strings. If you need to walk away from the instrument, carefully lay it on its side and put the endpin in. For more information on the endpin, see **Tip 17**.

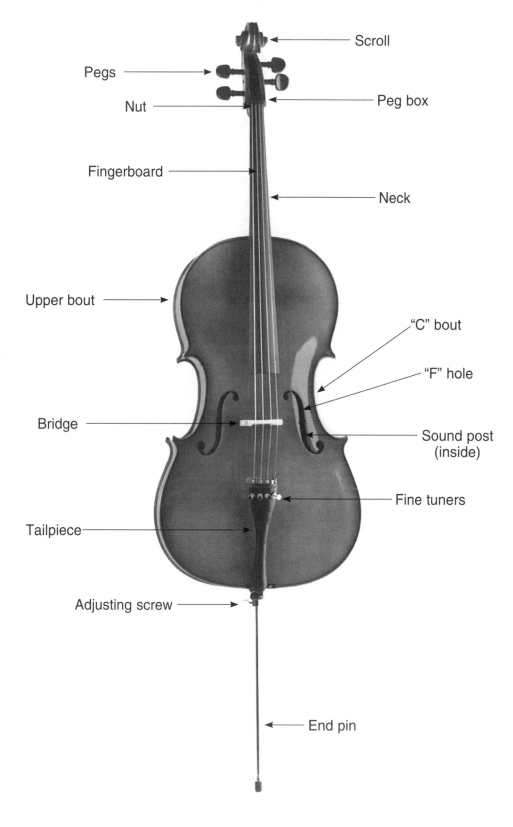

Scroll

Pegs

Nut

Peg box

Fingerboard

Neck

Upper bout

"C" bout

"F" hole

Bridge

Sound post (inside)

Fine tuners

Tailpiece

Adjusting screw

End pin

 **STRINGS**

(YOU GET WHAT YOU PAY FOR)

A set of cello strings can cost from about $50.00 to more than $150.00. Shop around for strings to find the best prices at your local music dealers.

Because of the variety of materials available in the core and the winding of the strings, cellists often combine different brands of strings. For example, one recommended combination is to have Jargar A and D strings with Dominant G and C strings. Another good combination is Larsen A and D strings with Helicore G and C strings. Medium tension is the most common.

3 STRINGS: INSTALLATION

When replacing a string, you must first remove the old one (you knew that). Next, turn the fine tuner down several turns and apply graphite (pencil) to the groove at the nut, bridge, and fine tuner. This helps keep the string lubricated to prevent breakage. Bend the top of the string at a right angle about a centimeter from the top (see Fig. 1). Prop the cello between your knees facing you, and thread the top into the corresponding peg from above. When winding, make sure the string doesn't cross over itself in the peg box (see Fig. 2). Wind it gradually toward the outside of the peg box. Hold the string in place and hook it at the tailpiece (in the fine tuner if you have one, otherwise in the tailpiece hole). Before the string has a pitch (when it's still loose and floppy), line it up with the bridge notch and tighten slowly. Do not turn the string higher than the proper pitch, but gradually approach from below. If your string keeps breaking at the same spot, check with a repair shop.

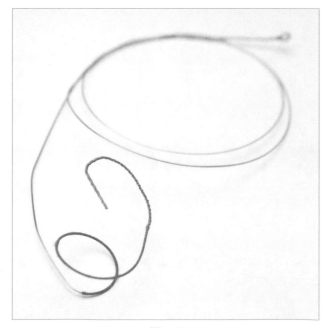

Fig. 1

Fig. 2

4 BRIDGE MATTERS

The shape of the bridge should follow the curve of your fingerboard. Some fingerboards have a section cut away under the C string to give more room for the C string to vibrate. A more ornately carved bridge will have a better sound, but will need more maintenance.

If your bridge warps, it will need fixing. While you might want to leave this to a repairman, if you have strong fingertips, you can adjust your own bridge. Watch the bridge feet to make sure they don't move. Push at the top of the bridge until it is straighter. You may need to make small adjustments to the bridge a few times. If it is very warped, it may need to be sanded down or replaced. Pressing gently down on the top of the bridge with your fingertips when you need to tighten the peg can help prevent warping.

The bridge feet should be placed between the notches of the f-holes on the front panel. The bridge should be straight up from the feet, or a bit further back, away from the fingerboard. If your bridge was removed or replaced, check for markings on the cello front where the bridge feet were originally set. (Some cellos have a bridge with moveable feet, which allows it to fit with any cello front.)

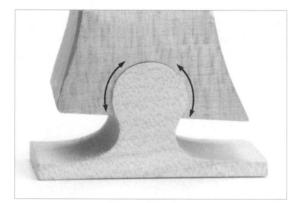

Moveable foot

Changes in humidity can affect the instrument and bridge to the point that some cellists use different bridges for winter and summer. Since wood expands with humidity in the summer (imagine how a door sticks), summer bridges are often a bit shorter than their winter counterparts.

5 ACTION: NUT TO BRIDGE
(FINGERS HAPPY)

Playing on a cello with a bridge that is too high can be painful. Check the playing **action** (string height) at the nut and the bridge. Have an experienced player check if the action is too high. If the action is too low, the strings will go flat or buzz against the fingerboard when you play in high positions. Sometimes the action is faulty only on the A- or C-string end of the bridge. Play in the full range of the cello to make sure the action doesn't compromise certain pitches. The string notches should be evenly spaced (like on the front cover) across the bridge top with the strings resting on top of the bridge. If the notches are at the correct depth, the strings will feel like bumps on top of the bridge. If the strings are sunken into the notches, the bridge could be shaved down a bit so the notches aren't so deep. Try this first before you replace your bridge.

BOWS: WOOD VS. FIBERGLASS
(CARBON FIBER, TOO)

A professional player usually plays with a wood bow which has a high-quality Pernambuco stick. The lesser wood bows are made of Brazilwood. The cheapest beginner-level bow is commonly made of fiberglass. Another option for a student-level bow, or one that can be used when playing in alternative (non-classical) styles is a durable carbon fiber stick.

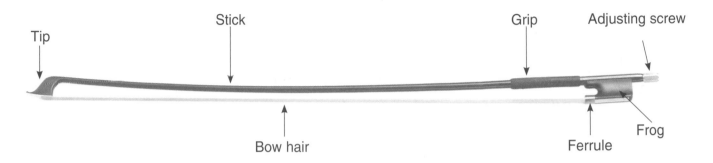

 # HORSEHAIR OR SYNTHETIC?

Horsehair is far superior in tone to synthetic. Since horsehair is more expensive, a good student-level option is a fiberglass stick with real horsehair. In general, the higher quality bows have Mother of Pearl trim on the frog, a leather grip, and metal winding, while a lesser-quality bow will have a plastic grip and no winding. The photo to the right offers a close-up view of the parts of a higher quality bow.

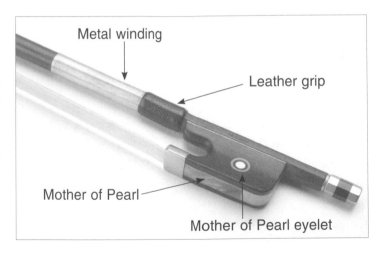

8 BOW CARE

Tighten the bow before playing by turning the adjusting screw at the bottom of the bow three to five times. Always loosen the bow when you are finished playing. When tight, the hair should be away from the stick at about the width of your index finger. If the bow stick is not slightly curved in the middle toward the hair, your bow is too tight or the stick is warped. Avoid touching the bow hair—natural skin oils will ruin the rosin retention. Periodically wipe the stick clean of rosin, but don't bother cleaning the rosin off the bow hair, only to add rosin later. If a hair comes loose, carefully cut it off with scissors. Ripping the hair out of the bow can cause more hairs to loosen.

The bow needs to be rehaired (all of the hair removed and new hair installed) according to use. Professional players often have their bow rehaired every six months, while students may rehair once a year, or every other year, depending on how much one can afford. After your bow has been rehaired, the hair should be spread all the way across the ferrule.

9 ROSIN: DARK AND LIGHT

Rosin is a resin used on the bow hair to create friction on the strings. Packaged in cakes, rosin is necessary for the string to make a sound. Wipe rosin on the bow hair about every other time you play. A new bow may need more rosin. While being applied, rosin will lighten the bow hair. To avoid excess rosin dust, swipe the last few strokes in the same direction on the hair. Keep your rosin on the floor or in your case, not on a music stand. If rosin falls on the floor, it can crumble into many useless pieces.

The darker the rosin, the softer the consistency will be. Since violin rosin is usually lighter and bass rosin darker (and therefore softer), cello rosin can range between light amber, red, and dark green. Cellists should avoid very light violin rosin, or dark bass rosin. Beware: very soft rosin can melt out of its shape in the summer. Some better rosin brands include Hill, Pirastro, Andrea, Millant-Deroux, and Jade.

Cooking tip: Rosin that has cracked into pieces can be wrapped in tin foil and baked in the oven. Although this can save you money by salvaging that cracked cake of rosin, it can stink up a whole house. Warning: Some rosin cakes come in a very flammable wrap.

TUNING: HAVE A REFERENCE
(AND BE CAREFUL)

Many players use a tuner, pitch pipe, or keyboard as a reference. The cello is tuned to A, D, G, and C from top to bottom. The A string is the first A below middle C on a keyboard. It is recommended you use a tuner, tuning fork, or keyboard for the A string only, then try to tune the rest by ear like the professionals. You can check after you're done with the keyboard or tuner. Try humming or singing the pitches for ear training.

Turning the pegs for the first time can be dangerous. First turn the corresponding fine tuner down (counter-clockwise) several turns. Then turn the peg down (toward you) until you hear a clicking sound. Next slowly turn the peg up to the proper pitch while plucking the string with your other thumb. Do not let go of the peg until you have made it stick into the peg box. Never turn the peg up without first loosening.

Stuck peg tip: If you really can't turn that stuck peg at all, wrap a cloth around the peg and carefully use pliers over the cloth to turn the peg down.

Slipping pegs: "Peg dope" is a waxy substance which you apply to the tuning peg where it meets the peg box. It increases friction and prevents slipping.

Loosen

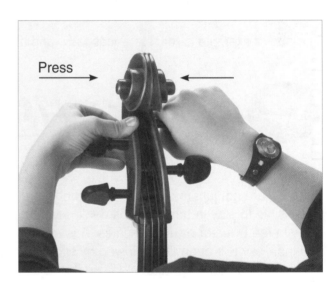

Tighten

The following example shows the open-string notes on the staff. Tune these carefully, starting with the A as notated. Use the A at the beginning of the audio track as a reference to tune your A, then stop the audio track and tune each of your strings by ear. When finished, play the entire track to hear all open strings and play along, checking your pitches against the audio track.

Reference A

11 TUNING WITH DOUBLE STOPS

Most violinists and violists tune their strings by playing **double-stops** (two strings at the same time). This is only successful if the ear can hear the interval of a **perfect fifth** (see **Tip 12**). First make sure your A string is in tune. Play it alone for a long time, letting the pitch settle in your ear. Then play the A and D strings at the same time. If you hear a "wah–wah" sound, you are hearing the sound waves. This means the strings are close, but not quite in tune. If you can't tell if the D is sharp (too high) or flat (too low), experiment by trial and error. If the sound waves disappear and it sounds in tune, double-check it with your tuner or keyboard. The same process can be repeated with D and G-strings, followed by G and C. The problem with tuning open fifths ("open" as in open strings) using double stops is that the ear tends to hear chords from the bottom up. Your ear may perceive the D string to be in tune even when you have tuned the A string first. Students need to go slowly. Every player should take enough time to listen carefully and improve their ear.

The above example is for references only, and not meant to be played "in time."

12 PERFECT FIFTHS: TWINKLE TEST

Intervals are not just matters of music theory, separate from playing. If you can't hear intervals, it is impossible to play in tune—cellos don't have frets. The interval between D up to A is called a **perfect fifth**. In the D major or minor scales, A is the fifth scale degree. The cello, violin, and viola are tuned in fifths. Play two open Ds, followed by two open As. It should sound like the beginning of "Twinkle, Twinkle, Little Star." You can also use this "Twinkle test" by starting on two Gs followed by two Ds, or two Cs followed by two Gs.

⓭ HARMONICS FOR TUNING

If you lightly touch (don't press down) at the exact halfway point on any string, it will sound an octave higher than the open string. This higher pitch is a **harmonic**. To get a good ringing harmonic, put your left thumb at the "heel" (where the neck meets the back of the cello) and stretch your ring finger out over the fingerboard. You may need to fish around with your finger to find the spot where the harmonic really rings. Sometimes just leaning your finger back or forward can help you find the pitch. Harmonics sound best with a fast bow stroke. Try this on the A string. Next, bring out the thumb and place it on the D string at a fifth above open D (the note A on the D string). The same pitch should be produced on the A string with your third (ring) finger (on the halfway point) as on the D string with your thumb, thus you can compare these two notes to see if they are in tune with each other. Use the same part of the bow, and the same bow direction between the strings. A down-bow starting at the frog can sound very different from an up-bow starting from the tip. The table below may be helpful in tuning with harmonics. "3" indicates the third finger harmonic (finger at the halfway point on the string). "T" indicates the thumb (resting on the string a fifth up from the open-string note). The "0" is a reminder that the string is technically still "open," because you're not pressing down on the string, rather just touching the string.

3	T		3	T		3	T
0	0		0	0		0	0
on A = on D			on D = on G			on G = on C	

This audio track demonstrates tuning the cello using harmonics, starting with the A string, then the D string, followed by the G, then C. When you tune your cello, do not tune to all the notes on this audio track demonstration. Only tune to the reference pitch and then do the rest on your own, using your ears.

14 HARMONICS
(NATURAL VS. ARTIFICIAL)

Natural harmonics can be found at certain fractional spots on any string (1/2, 1/3, 1/4, and 1/5) such as the halfway point discussed in the previous tip. Artificial harmonics require an additional finger to stop the string. Cellists use the index finger or thumb to stop the string (as if fingering a note), then lightly add the pinky or third finger one-fourth above the stopped point. Some artificial harmonics require a big stretch of the left hand.

15 CELLO BRANDS

The best cellos are handmade by professional luthiers, who are also called "violin makers." Don't worry, like Amati, they can also make a great cello as well as a violin. Some standard student-level brands of stringed instruments include Meisel, Klaus Mueller, Kroger, Hoffmann, Engelhardt, Strunal, Glaesel/ Sherl & Roth, and Knilling. Upper-level brands include Eastman, Yuan Qin, Han Kroger, and Scott Cao, but these are only a few of what's out there. If you have a favorite cellist, you could go on the internet, find out what kind of instrument they play, and check it out. However, what works for a musician you admire may not be right for you; but still, it's a starting point.

16 BUYING A CELLO

A high-quality instrument will be hard carved instead of laminated (it will have a more flat finish as opposed to being shiny or glossy). It will also have nice flaming (looks like stripes) on the back panel. Keep in mind that you get what you pay for. Ask if that low price is for a whole outfit (includes bow and case). Some outfits also include a rockstop, rosin, polish, and a cleaning cloth. You will also need a humidifier for winter. Have a knowledgeable string player look at and even play the different instruments for you. A new cello will have a bright sound, but will develop a more mellow sound over time. An older instrument may have more maintenance issues. Find out how old the pegs and bridge are, and what work was recently done.

Purfling is the outline on the cello's front panel that follows the outer edge of the cello like an outline. The purfling is actually different pieces of wood wedged in the panel to protect the cello. If the edge gets cracked, the purfling can stop the crack from spreading across the panel. The worst quality stringed instruments will have painted on purfling instead of inlaid purfling. You can see the brush strokes at the corners of the bouts.

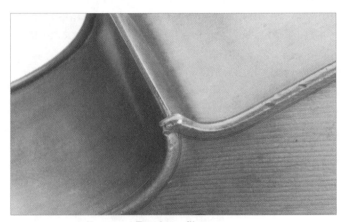

Real purfling

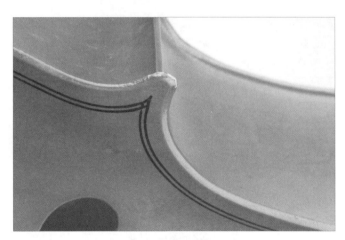

Painted purfling

17 ENDPIN TROUBLE

The endpin anchors the cello to the floor. When shopping for a cello, check the length of the endpin. If the cellist is a growing student, make sure the endpin has extra length. A good measurement for setting your endpin out for playing is your hand span (from thumb to pinky) plus a couple inches. If the upper bout corner of the cello is touching your left thigh, the endpin is too short. Also check to make sure the C string peg is behind the left ear.

Notches on an endpin tend to be unreliable. Even when the endpin is properly tightened, the cello can fall down over the endpin while the unfortunate cellist is playing—no notches please!

A **rock stop** (also called an end pin rest) is a small rubber device with a hole in the middle for the endpin. Shaped like a hockey puck, it keeps the cello from slipping. Nine or ten dollars is worth the piece of mind. If you are stuck without a rockstop, you could either get out your electric drill and damage the floor, or put your shirt (or ladies, your soft case) under a leg of your chair and stretch it out to the end of the endpin.

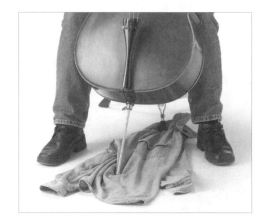

18 MUTES

A mute, placed directly on the bridge, gives any instrument a softer, muffled tone. The most common cello mutes are made of ebony, metal, or rubber, costing from $4.00 to about $13.00. Many players store their mute on the string close to the tailpiece. The indication in music for using the mute is **con sordino**. **Senza sordino** instructs the player to remove their mute. The very large practice mute can be handy if you need to practice in a hotel or warm up backstage.

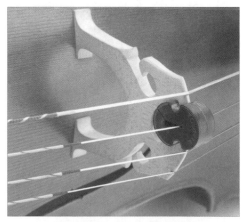

Rubber mute on G string

From L to R: Practice mute, metal mute, rubber mute (tourte style)

The following scale is played twice: first time without the mute, and the second time with the mute. Listen for the difference in **timbre** (tone color).

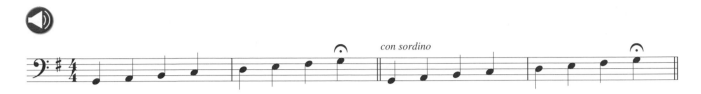

Use of the mute is even more pronounced when used by an entire section of string instruments as in an orchestra playing Claude Debussy's "Nuages."

19 BIG BAD WOLF TONE

An unfortunate sympathetic vibration is common in the middle range of the cello, often at E♭, E, or F. It is called a **wolf tone** because of the growling sound it produces. A **dewolfer** (wolf eliminator) is basically a rubber mute that can be attached to the string, usually the G. It has a small screw on it (like your fine tuner) that eliminates the sound. Placing a small mute on the G-string about a centimeter from the bridge is a cheaper alternative to the dewolfer if you are willing to spend the time to find the exact spot where it eliminates the tone.

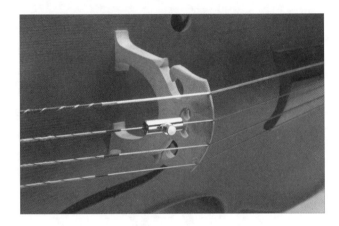

20 CASES

Most soft cases are less expensive than hard. A bow pocket that runs straight down outside the fingerboard is better than a pocket to the side of the bridge, which may cause the bow to warp. Young players can easily put on and carry cases that have backpack straps. Make sure you take the bow out first when unpacking the cello, and put it in last. Young students can be told that the bow hates to be in the case—this way it won't be broken when the case gets taken off the cello. The best soft cello case will have many reinforced pockets and plenty of foam padding, such as the Kaces Cello Bag.

While hard cases are best to protect the cello from the elements, they are much heavier than soft cases. If you're going to buy a hard case, get one with wheels and multiple handles and straps (back pack straps can help with a long stair climb). If you have a pet that sheds, reconsider your cello case covering—canvas may attract pet hair. Dependable hard cases include Bam, SKB, Bobelock, and Meisel.

21 CLEANING AND POLISHING

To avoid rosin build up and a compromised tone, the cello strings should always be scrubbed with a soft cloth after playing. Rubbing alcohol can get serious grit off the string, but be careful not to get alcohol on the front panel of the cello. Wipe fingerprints off of the cello surfaces with a soft cloth (cotton or silk). Use instrument polish on the cello about every sixth months. Do not let the cello come in contact with water, alcohol, or furniture polish.

If you have students, insist that they wash their hands before playing. Check how often their cleaning cloth gets washed.

22 SITTING POSTURE

Proper cello posture includes sitting on the front half of the chair with both feet flat on the floor, and your back straight. Your rockstop should make an isosceles triangle on the floor with your feet. The fingers on both hands should be curved, like you are holding a soft ball. The wrists on both hands should be straight.

Sitting for a long time on the edge of a chair will be difficult at first. Take breaks when practicing, and try to "sit tall" (as if you are standing). Keep your rib cage up, but the shoulders back. Don't change your regular neck or head posture for playing the cello. Instead, bring the cello to your body.

Ladies: If you must wear a skirt, make sure it is a long, full skirt. If the miniskirt is a staple of your wardrobe, have a pair of shorts along to avoid a possible wardrobe malfunction. That goes for upper string players too.

Rest position

Playing position

23 LEFT-HAND SHAPE

The fingers on the left hand should have about a centimeter of space between them. The thumb should be across from the second finger (middle finger). Most beginners put as many fingers down as possible while playing. For example, when using third finger, their first and second fingers are also down, helping hold down the string. If your hand is too small to reach between B and D on the A string, you may need to pivot. This means not putting all four fingers down at once when using the pinky. If the pinky is too weak to hold down the string alone, try putting third and fourth finger down together when using pinky. Eventually your fingers should get strong enough to put one finger down at a time.

24 A GOOD BOW HOLD
(RIGHT-HAND SHAPE)

Flop all four fingers over the bow stick as if they are very heavy. The thumb should be slightly bent, with its tip on the hill of the frog. If your thumb and second finger are fighting for space, you may be jamming the thumb too far into the bow. Curl the index and second finger around the stick and place the thumb between your second and third fingers. The most popular beginning bow hold is to put the thumb under the stick, on the ferrule. With either bow hold, make sure your thumb is perpendicular to the bow stick. The thumb should be bent a bit (or a lot if you are double-jointed), but not bent backwards. For a powerful tone, do not let your wrist rise above the arm or knuckles. Since the balance point is the string, check your bow hold by holding it up toward the ceiling or once the bow is resting on the string.

Bow hold: front view

Bow hold: behind view

Bow hold: beginning

25 DOWN-BOW, UP-BOW

The "**down-bow**" marking (⊓) indicates to pull the bow to the right, usually starting at the frog. The "**up-bow**" marking (∨) indicates to pull to the left, starting in the upper half of the bow. Since bow markings are confusing when playing on the A string (you pull up in the air for a down-bow, and in an up-bow, the direction is actually down toward the floor), think about bow direction on your C string: down-bow is down, up-bow is up. Or, remember that your right hand is always by the bridge to start a down-bow.

Bowing Logic Tip: Since the frog is the heaviest part of the bow, the down-bow stroke is louder. This is why down-bow is usually for notes on the beat, while an up-bow is used for pickup notes. Uniform bowing within a string section helps keep the articulation the same. If you play in a section and don't bother to use the correct bowing, the audience will assume that you are the one making the mistakes!

26 SLURS INDICATE BOWING

A **slur** is used to indicate when two or more notes are played within the same bow stroke. In music notation, a horizontal arc above or below the included notes indicates a slur. When practicing multiple notes in one bow stroke, begin with just two notes, and work your way up to playing string crossing slurs (between different strings), and then entire scales in one bow stroke (as in the last example below). A tie is executed the same as a slur. While a slur has different pitches, a tie connects two notes of the same pitch.

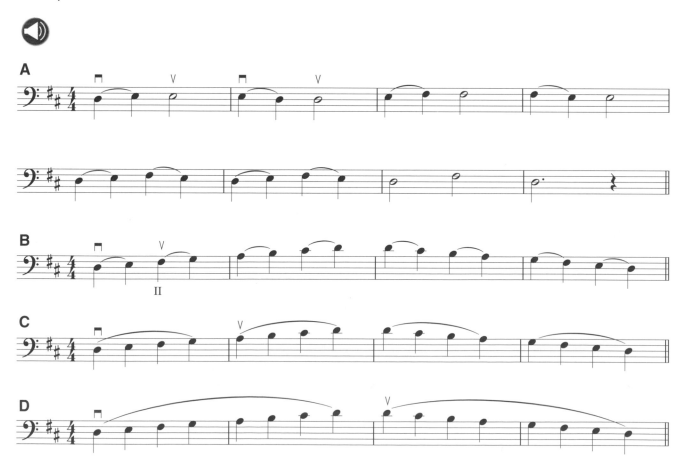

27 HOOKED BOWING

A **hooked bowing** notation looks like a slur when notated, but with dots above or below the note heads. A hooked bowing has multiple notes in the same bow direction like a slur, but with stops in the bow movement for each note. The result sounds like separate bow strokes. A common use for the hooked bowing is to emphasize the downbeat, such as beat one in a minuet. If you introduce hooks to a young student, make sure they understand that a dot next to the note head (like the dotted half note in measure 8 below) changes the rhythm, while a dot above or below changes only the articulation.

Minuet 1

Johann Sebastian Bach

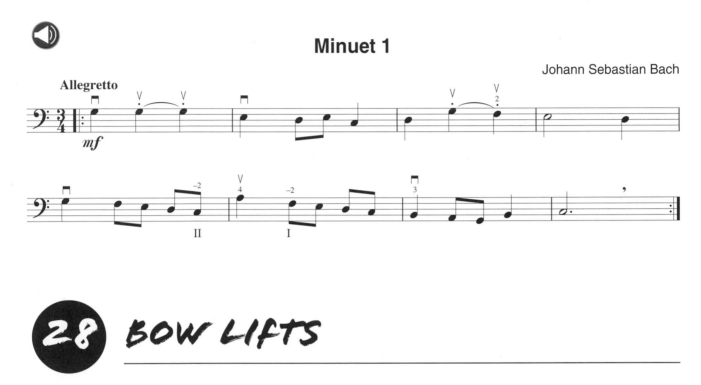

28 BOW LIFTS

A **bow lift** is usually put between two down-bow markings. The object of a bow lift is to return the bow to its original spot on the string. Also called a **circle-bow**, because the bow literally makes a circle in the air. The bow lift is technically an up-bow in the air, enabling the player to do successive down-bows for a heavy, powerful sound. The symbol for a bow lift is an apostrophe above the staff. For wind players, the bow lift marking is used as a breath mark.

Au Clair de la Lune

French Folksong

On beat 4 of measure 2, lift the bow, making a circle in the air to return it to a "near the frog" position on the string. This gets the bow ready to play down-bow on beat 1 of measure 3.

29 PLAYING COL LEGNO

Col legno is an Italian term directing string players to use the wood, or stick of the bow, instead of the hair. This is a special-effect sound, one that can be ethereal and mysterious. It is also fairly quiet compared to bowing with the hair.

Composers will also often ask players to bounce the stick off the string when playing *col legno*. Unless you play really hard it should not harm the bow stick. Wipe the stick clean of rosin immediately after playing *col legno*.

This audio track first demonstrates *col legno* using bow strokes, then a few notes bouncing the bow on the strings.

30 SUL PONTICELLO

Sul ponticello is another Italian term, indicating a special-effect bowing style. In this technique, the bow is in contact with the strings very close to and can be even on top of the bridge. This glassy, somewhat harsh sound is often done by accident by beginners, to the woe of anyone within earshot. You can achieve this unique sound by bowing less than a centimeter away from the bridge. Experiment with how close the bow gets to the bridge to hear the changes in timbre. Use this technique next time you're in a suspenseful mood.

sul ponticello

31 SUL TASTO

Sul tasto means to play over the fingerboard, away from the bridge. It facilitates playing at a softer volume without changing bow pressure. *Sul tasto* can also be used for prolonged double stops, because the space between the strings lessens the further the bow is away from the bridge.

sul tasto

32 BOUNCING THE BOW
(SPICCATO, JETE, ETC.)

Various techniques are used in which the bow is off the string. Find the balance point of your bow. This is where it should be placed on the string to begin bouncing, or **spiccato**. Start with the bow on the string, and pull off into the air. Like dribbling a basketball, spiccato is easier if you keep it bouncing. Spiccato is also known as **sautille**, **saltando**, or **saltato**. **Jete** (also called ricochet) is similar to throwing the bow on the string from above, letting it bounce repeatedly in one stroke. Controlling the rebounds is the challenge when using any bouncing technique.

Both "Surprise Symphony Theme" and "Eine Kleine Nachtmusik" employ the use of spiccato playing, primarily on short and staccato notes.

Surprise Symphony Theme

Franz Josef Haydn

Eine Kleine Nachtmusik
Movement I

Wolfgang Amadeus Mozart

33 TREMOLO

Tremolo effect is achieved by bowing as fast as possible in very short strokes. The bow can move faster at the tip or upper half of the bow. This sound effect is characteristic of stringed instruments building tension in horror/suspense movie soundtracks. Keep a loose wrist and hand when playing tremolo. Your elbow should be almost completely motionless. In notation, *tremolo* is indicated by three short lines above or below a note. One or two slashes does not mean tremolo, but can indicate doubled or quadrupled bowing.

34 BEGINNING VIBRATO

Vibrato consists of small, even fluctuations (bends) of the pitch. For string players, the arm or hand shakes, causing the finger to move while pressing on the string. Cello vibrato is similar to the motion your arm and hand make when opening a doorknob. Strong fingers are a prerequisite for vibrato. Vibrato on the lower stringed instruments (cello and bass) is easier than on violin and viola, since we don't have to hold up the instrument with the same arm that does vibrato. Make sure that you are using only one finger of the left hand at a time. Since the third and fourth fingers tend to be the weakest, spend time using them alone prior to working on vibrato.

Pre-vibrato exercise:

In third or fourth position, grab all the way around the cello neck. Keeping the other fingers down (you may need to use the right hand to hold down the other fingers), make small independent vibrato motions with each finger.

Play a fingered note without any vibrato. Begin sliding the finger up and down on the string, letting your whole hand move together. Next, put the thumb in place behind the neck, and isolate the finger movement.

Teaching tip: "Polishing" the string is a quiet exercise where your thumb stays put and your finger moves up and down on the string without any right-hand bowing.

Begin with a very slow, exaggerated vibrato. You can speed it up gradually. If you speed it up too quickly, vibrato will sound tight and nervous. This audio track plays the same melody twice: first without vibrato, then with a standard or "normal" vibrato.

Once you are comfortable with vibrato, vibrate immediately when you start a note. However, in certain musical passages with long notes, it may be effective to start out a note with no vibrato, and then employ it later in the duration (see **Tip 35**).

Many players have coordination problems when they begin vibrating and bowing. Try playing *pizzicato* (plucked) when using vibrato. Some players find it beneficial to take the thumb away from the neck when starting vibrato. A disadvantage of this method is that the cellist may only be able to do vibrato this way if he/she delays moving the thumb back to the neck.

35 VIBRATO DO'S & DON'TS

If you do not play well in tune, you are not ready for vibrato. Don't try to speed up the vibrato before it feels relaxed. While vibrato is required for music of the Classical and Romantic eras, it is used less in the Baroque and Renaissance. Many contemporary and jazz musicians will vary their vibrato speed, or use vibrato as an effect.

In playing a passage of music, be careful not to use the same vibrato on every note. Try to use the vibrato differently according to phrasing, varying its use so as not to sound too mechanical. For example, some notes may be affected by a faster, deeper vibrato, while other notes only use a lighter vibrato toward the end of their duration. One example would be to start out a phrase with light vibrato, and with each note, the vibrato gets deeper and more intense into the middle of the phrase. Then, as the phrase starts coming to an end, back off on the vibrato gradually.

Experiment with starting a pitch without vibrato, and add in a slow vibrato gradually as on the second note on the next audio track. This is called "warming it up." You can also try speeding up the vibrato gradually, and then slowing it down gradually, all over the course of one long note. Many players use varying vibrato speeds for expression, so feel free to experiment. Use varying speeds and degrees of vibrato as techniques of expression to suit different types of music.

36 PLAYING IN TUNE
(MARKERS AND INTERVALS)

Since the cello is fretless, most beginners need help knowing where to place the fingers to play in tune. Teachers often put tape on the fingerboard for the first, third, and fourth fingers. If you want to be more discreet, use clear tape. Another option is to lightly mark the fingerboard with chalk or graphite, which wears off quickly. If you want to leave the fingerboard alone, place a small piece of tape or sticker on the back of the cello neck for the thumb (across from where your second finger belongs). Reinforcers for three-hole binder paper work well and are inexpensive.

Perfect fourth: Players who want to get their fourth finger in tune can check their perfect fourth from an open string to adding the pinky. If you play open D followed by fourth finger on D (which will sound the G above), it is a perfect fourth. It should sound like the beginning of the familiar "Here Comes the Bride" melody.

37 PHYSICS OF PLAYING IN TUNE

Playing in tune is a combination of knowing what the sound should be before playing, responding, and knowing the tendency of your instrument and physicality. In other words, listen.

Sympathetic vibration, also called "ringing tone," is a string vibrating when you play its note name, even in a different octave. For example, if you play a D on the C string, your open D string will vibrate if your finger is in the right spot. Play an A on your G-string, and the open A-string should vibrate. Every A, D, G, and C on the cello, when fingered, should cause this ringing tone. Sympathetic vibrations can be beneficial to playing in tune, especially with the index and fourth fingers. When you're playing a D, if it is in tune, the sympathetic ringing of the open D string should be noticeable—the D you're playing should sound more full and resonant.

Use this method for getting notes in tune when you start shifting. For example, in fourth position on the D string, your first finger should make A vibrate and the pinky should get the C string ringing. Because of their thicker gauge, the string vibrations are most easily observable on the lower strings. For more on shifting, see **Tip 39**.

If you know what pitch to expect before pulling the bow, you will be able to adjust faster to get it in tune. The best players make immediate adjustments because they are listening and know the piece. They are able to hear the pitch in their head before they have to play it. Listen to recordings of pieces you are learning to help develop your ear.

Be aware of your hand shape. The thumb often causes many problems with both hands. Before playing or after rests, always check the placement of both thumbs.

Cellists tend to play with a flat pinky. If you stretch out your fingers and notice that there is a lot more space between the second and third finger, your second finger may tend to be flat and the third finger sharp.

Cellists have to stretch farther on the G and C strings than on the A and D. Players who first begin using extensions usually don't stretch far enough. For an extended index finger (E♭ on the D string), point your finger back toward the nut. For an extended pinky (C♯ on the G string), point your pinky toward the floor. Players call the extended index finger "low one," and the extended fourth finger "high four."

E♭ extension

C♯ extension

38 SCALES ARE LIKE VEGETABLES

Although scales and etudes (technical studies) may be a musician's least favorite to practice, they are good for your playing.

Scales make your fingers and ears familiar with different modes and keys. Scale passages are common in music and can be practiced with different rhythms for variety. It is more practical to spend your time learning scales well in one octave at a time than being able to run up and down your cello in four octaves at once. Scale passages in music are rarely more than an octave. To be a versatile player, work on major, natural minor, melodic minor, and harmonic minor scales, as well as the blues scale.

Can-Can

Jacques Offenbach
Arr. John Higgins

You may already be familiar with some of the different modes. For example, the **Ionian mode** is the same as the major scale, and **Aeolian** is the same as the natural minor. To learn different modes starting on any pitch, reference the whole- and half-step sequences listed below: Dorian, Phrygian, Lydian, Mixolydian, Aeolian, and Locrian).

Mode	Whole (W) and Half Steps (h) in ascending order						
Ionian	W	W	h	W	W	W	h
Dorian	W	h	W	W	W	h	W
Phrygian	h	W	W	W	h	W	W
Lydian	W	W	W	h	W	W	h
Mixolydian	W	W	h	W	W	h	W
Aeolian	W	h	W	W	h	W	W
Locrian	h	W	W	h	W	W	W

These modes are also useful for improvisation. Consult a jazz text on the use of scales and modes in improvisation. (Yes, cellists can play jazz.)

③⑨ SHIFTING: SLIDE, DON'T JUMP

Shifting on the cello is difficult because going higher on the fingerboard is unfamiliar and shifting back to first position is going against gravity. When violinists and violists shift higher, their left hand moves closer to their face and they get a better view of their fingers.

When shifting, keep your thumb moving lightly along with your hand as one unit. Some players slide a finger up the fingerboard then add the finger to be used for the ultimate pitch at the very end of the shift. For example, if you need to shift on the A string from B in first position to the B an octave higher, shift your hand to the needed position, play the harmonic A with the second finger, and add third finger, which is ready for the B. Most of the mistakes in shifting result from not hearing the pitch ahead of time, and physically not shifting far enough, producing a flat pitch. A certain fear is present when you can't hear the pitch ahead of time and so you may end up playing a kind of guessing game, reaching up into unfamiliar territory. This fear and worry can often result in a weak tone which only adds to the possible intonation problem. To overcome this when shifting, remember to listen, breathe, and stay strong with the bow.

Plan Ahead

Where will your hand and elbow end up after the shift? Lighten the weight of your hand just before shifting. Try a sliding shift in which you **glissando** (slide) up or down between the two notes. When figuring out when to shift in a piece, try not to shift three notes in a row, or use the same finger three times. If a difficult shift is giving you trouble, try playing it backwards. To make sure you are really listening, close your eyes.

④⓪ PIZZICATO: CLASSICAL VS. JAZZ

The Italian term **pizzicato** (abbreviated **pizz.**) indicates for the player to pluck the string with the right hand. The traditional classical pizzicato style is to draw the sound out of the string in an upward motion. By using the side of the finger and as much flesh as possible, cellists can pull the string sideways in a jazz style for a walking bass line (much like an upright bass plays).

For long pizzicato endurance, many players alternate between the first two or three fingers of the right hand (the index finger is most common). For more volume, pluck close to the bridge and use the first and second fingers together like one big finger.

The next example shows a cello duet for the tune "Dance of the Hours." Both cellos play pizzicato.

Dance of the Hours

Amilcare Ponchielli

The following features the jazz-style *pizz.* and shows how a cellist can function much like a jazz bass player.

Jazz Pizzicato

41 LEFT-HAND PIZZICATO

Left hand pizzicato is sometimes a necessity if there is not enough time to switch from *arco*, and the last pizzicato note is an open string. It is also used as a special effect in between *arco* notes, to show off the player's virtuosity. Left-hand pizzicato is most often done with the pinky. In the following example, "+" signs are used to indicate pizzicato.

Left-Hand Pizzicato

42 BARTÓK PIZZICATO

Also called a **snap pizz.**, the **Bartók pizz.** has a history with composer Béla Bartók, whose writing was influenced by Hungarian folk music. The snap *pizz.* is indicated in music with a special sign above the note (shown in the following musical example), often accompanied by a "sforzando" marking, a directive to perform the note with strong emphasis. It is accomplished by plucking the string high off the fingerboard, hard enough to make it snap back. While it does not harm the instrument, repeated snap *pizz.* can pull the string out of tune. For more about the amazing Béla Bartók, read *The Music of Béla Bartók* by Elliott Antokoletz (University of California Press).

Bartók Pizzicato

This percussive sound is also particularly effective when an entire cello section does it. This effect is common in movie soundtracks

43 STRUMMING CHORDS

Some cellists play chords with their fingers or a guitar pick. Use a hard pick since the cello strings are thicker than guitar strings. Players most commonly pluck chords with their thumb from the bottom up. Because the cello is fretless, playing chords well in tune can be problematic. Try strumming only two of the pitches, and get them in tune before adding the third, then fourth pitch. Lindsay Mac is a well-known cellist who uses a lot of pizzicato and strumming in her style.

Strumming Chords

44 ALTERNATIVE STYLES

The world of alternative string playing has been expanding into folk and jazz, and more recently fusion and rock. Although the violin and bass have been in a variety of genres for a long time, the cello is catching up. Players such as Matt Turner, David Darling, Yo-Yo Ma, Steven Katz, Corbin Keep, Matt Haimovitz, Chris White, and ensembles like the Turtle Island String Quartet, Kronos Quartet, the Hampton String Quartet, and Apocalyptica have helped change the image of the cello. Check out the New Directions Cello Society and the Internet Cello Society for more nontraditional cellists. Their websites and many more are listed in **Tip 101**.

So the tip here is: Don't limit yourself to only classical music! The cello can play anything.

45 ELECTRIFY YOUR ACOUSTIC CELLO

Besides playing an electric cello, you can amplify your acoustic cello by attaching a pickup. Most acoustic pickups are fastened at the tailpiece with a cord that runs to the bridge. It attaches to the bridge with a small piece of copper. Many pickups have the standard quarter-inch jack. With a cable and pickup, you can plug into an amp and be as loud as any electric guitar.

Preamps

Unless you enjoy the harsh bow sounds amplified from the pickup (usually attached to the bridge), you need to use a preamp. Without a preamp, the tone in the upper range will sound very thin, and bow sounds are often too loud in the balance. Pick a preamp that has EQ options such as bass, treble, mid, and brilliance. Many companies that produce pickups also make a matching preamp. Fishman makes the most well-known pickups. You will probably need an extra cable and a 9-volt battery for the preamp. They are worth the hassle if you want a better amplified sound. Most electric cellos come with an internal preamp.

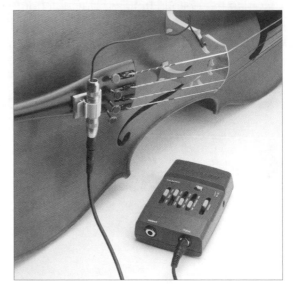

46 BUYING AN ELECTRIC CELLO

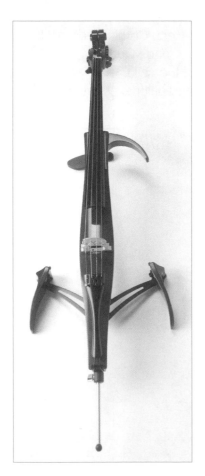

There are many options for brands of electric cellos. Like buying an acoustic, getting to play before you buy is important. The electric cello market is exploding, with some excellent instruments being made by NS Design, Starfish Designs, Vector, Violectra, Wood Violins (makes the Viper Cello), Yamaha (pictured), Zeta, and more. Many electric cellos have MIDI (Musical Instrument Digital Interface) inputs for recording, a headphone jack for silent practice, and the capability to play along with your favorite mobile device. Some stores will let you try out cellos in a practice room, or take it home for a few days before purchasing. Get the return policy in writing from a company before you buy their cello.

47 WHERE'S MY CELLO AMP?
(WHY YOU SHOULDN'T USE A GUITAR AMP)

Amplifier choice is very important. Unfortunately, most electric cellos don't come with their own custom amp. The cello has a lower range than guitar, so make sure it sounds good enough in its lowest range. The problem with a bass amp is that the cello has a great high range as well. Try different amps, including keyboard amps. Before purchasing an amp that sounds great at half volume, you need to test it at your performance volume.

Another important item to consider in choosing an amp is whether you'll be using it with an acoustic cello (with a pickup) or an electric cello. Acoustic instruments can feed back easily when the amp is turned up loud if you're using a standard keyboard, bass, or guitar amp. There are special amps made for acoustic instruments, designed to minimize feedback. The electric cello does not have this problem, but you may wish to use an amp with both your acoustic and electric cellos, so choose an amp that works well for both instruments. And when you're trying out an amp in the music store, don't be afraid to turn it up very loud. You'll want to test all volumes before you bring one home.

48 ONSTAGE: HEARING YOURSELF

The sounds you hear from your instrument (as well as how you hear other instruments around you) can be very different when playing in a cozy recital hall compared to a large concert hall, or that dive bar where you get your first rock gig. Your sound could end up dominating a string quartet (when it shouldn't) in that classical setting, or be completely obliterated by a drum set at a rock or jazz gig. Then add electric bass or keyboard, and you have lots of balance issues to consider. Always do your best to get in some playing time in whatever venue you'll be performing, before the actual performance. You need to be able to hear yourself, and predict how your instrument will sound within a group.

Ear damage tip: If you are listening to headphones (or ear buds) and someone else can hear the music a few feet away, it's too loud. Even if it doesn't bother your ears now, long-term exposure can also cause irreparable damage.

When your jazz combo or rock band is onstage, most players use earplugs. This is because they are smart people, who plan on being able to hear for many years. Earplugs can also help filter out excess background noise and actually help you hear the music better in loud rock-concert settings. In-ear monitors work like earplugs and a monitor together, but are expensive.

49 CELLO IN ROCK

Although the violin is better known in this genre, many rock groups are using cello. The genre of "Cello Rock" has now appeared on various music websites, including an entry on Wikipedia. Groups that are using cello as a regular instrument include After Crying, Alamaailman Vasarat, Apocalyptica, Break of Reality, Far Corner, Murder By Death, Rasputina, and Volapuk.

If you are the cellist in a rock group, know your role. Sometimes the cello is simply there as a rhythm instrument, or it may replace a keyboard or lead guitar. The incredible versatility of the cello also allows it to cover bass lines, vocal lines, or more percussive effects. Always make sure that the melody can be heard, no matter what the group's instrumentation.

50 CELLO AS LEAD VS. RHYTHM

Your role in the ensemble can be defined by your group's instrumentation. Sometimes the cellist functions as the lead guitar or vocal part, playing the melody. More often the cellist has a countermelody, or plays a more rhythmic role. If your part is like a rhythm guitar or bass, listen carefully to the drum set. Be aware of your volume, especially if you are being amplified. Crank the volume up (or change to a different sound effect) for a solo, and back off if you are just chopping or strumming chords.

51 MOVE WHEN YOU PLAY

Cello playing is hard on the human body, especially the parts that aren't moving. The shoulders, lower back, and legs often tense up during cello playing. Moving with the music—but not too much— helps enhance your performance, and lets oxygen get to your muscles (think blood flow). Watch the best players, and decide what works for your playing.

Fatigue Tip: String players can play for hours, as long as we take proper breaks. Beginners, especially older adults, need to stop if something hurts. Your left-hand fingertips may get sore, but as you keep practicing over a certain period of time, calluses will develop. A beginner should practice about twenty minutes per day. Break that time up into two ten-minute segments if necessary. For more practice ideas, check out **Tips 85** and **86**.

Treat your performance or rehearsal like an athletic event. Drink plenty of fluids, stretch before and after playing, and pace yourself.

52 EFFECTS PROCESSORS

While a guitar amp may not sound so good with your cello (especially if it's an acoustic), go ahead and borrow an effects processor from a guitar player. Or go to a music store and ask to try out a bunch of their guitar and bass pedals. Although their jaw may drop, the staff will be happy to help you, and curious to hear that cello with distortion. (That's right, along with your effects processor you will need another cable—and more available outlets.)

The following audio tracks in this tip are all recorded with an electric cello run through a guitar effects processor.

Distortion

Also called "overdrive," this audio track demonstrates cello with a guitar distortion effect applied.

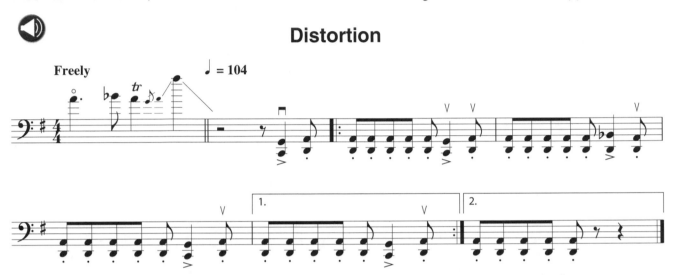

If you add any distortion to your sound, the effect makes articulation somewhat muddy. Your bow articulations must be shorter to give the same sounding length as your clean sound. This is similar to the orchestral (ensemble) staccato being shorter than the solo staccato. Work so you have a great spiccato and staccato, and your distorted sounds will be as well-articulated as your clean sound. An electric cellist can imitate the different effects that guitarists use with a pick or the fingers, but can also use the bow for endless possibilities.

Delay

Other great effects include chorus and delay. You can experiment with these effects in different combinations. The next audio track demonstrates chorus and a "ping-pong" delay. The **delay** is a kind of repeating echo, while the ping-pong effect causes each echo to bounce back and forth from the left channel to the right. Make sure you listen to this track on headphones to get the full effect.

Chorus

This effect causes a big stereo sound. It is often achieved by taking the original signal and having it slightly detuned in one channel compared to the other. Each channel can be panned far right and far left to increase the "big-ness" of the sound. The next audio track plays the same melody twice. The second time includes the chorus effect.

Reverb

You've been hearing reverb on every audio demo track. This effect puts your sound in a room so it does not sound dry. Reverbs can range from small rooms to large concert halls to even parking garages. If you listen carefully to the next track, you can hear the echo of the room, programmed to simulate different room sizes. The following excerpt is played three times. The first example demonstrates a **small room**; the second a **medium hall**; and the third a **large hall**.

Ave Verum Corpus
from K. 618

Wolfgang Amadeus Mozart

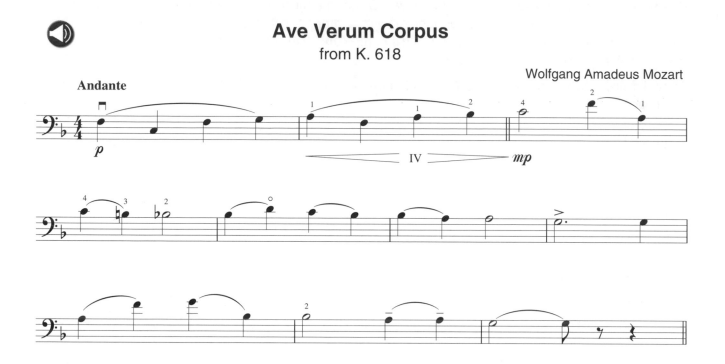

You can program many different kinds of reverb settings. Besides setting the size of the room, you can affect the reverb length, as well as adjust how much of the reverb signal you hear in relation to the original instrument signal. As a result, this enables you to control just how close the cello sounds. For example, sitting right next to a cello in a large church will sound different than sitting in the same church, but across the sanctuary from the cello.

Many players believe that effects such as chorus and reverb can help the overall sound. They are right, but don't overdo it. Record yourself playing with different effects and listen carefully. Sometimes it can sound good while you're playing, but you'll get a different perspective listening to a recording.

 53 EFFECTS PEDALS
(PRACTICE FOOT CONTROL)

If you are using an effects processor with pedals, make sure your floor setup enables you to see and reach the pedals with your right foot. Since most cellists sit, it's not easy to use those pedals. Also, cellists are not used to playing with pedals like guitar players are, so you need to incorporate your pedal usage into your practicing. This can be fun! Practice with whatever footwear you plan to record or perform with, so your pedal work is smooth. It may help to memorize sections of music around any pedal changes.

 54 INSTRUMENT SUBSTITUTE

The cello can function as the bass, guitar, or fiddle of a group. There are also percussive effects on the cello. The large, hollow body of the instrument can rest on your lap and be played like a drum. The swoops, scoops, and slides done by vocalists can be imitated with the bow. The cello is so versatile; the only limits are technique and imagination.

 55 COUNTRY-STYLE FIDDLE LICKS

There are fiddle groups out there who would welcome a cellist of any ability. If you are more of a beginner, stick to playing the bass lines, which often outline the chords. The slapping sound on off-beats of the bass line is done by simply slapping your hand on the strings.

Fiddle-style playing has a distinct use of the bow. There are many open strings and double stops. "Chopping" is playing at the frog, using small bow strokes (often consecutive down-bows) on the off beats. Fiddle players usually use a looser bow (less tightening of the adjusting screw) than classical, and often have a lower bridge to facilitate the double-stops. Experiment with using the upper half of the bow and less pressure like a fiddler on those tough passages.

There are also many fiddle pieces out there for an advanced cellist to tackle—you don't need to be stuck with the bass line. Put your treble clef reading abilities to the test and grab a violin part. If you don't know about the different clefs for cellists, read **Tips 63** through **65** first. Fiddle tunes are traditionally learned by ear and often have a simple form.

"Bile Them Cabbage Down" demonstrates some basic fiddle techniques. Besides the double stops as notated in the next example, listen to the audio track to hear other cello parts playing the off-beat slap as well as the bass line. You could form your own all-cello fiddle band!

Bile Them Cabbage Down

North American Fiddle Tune

56 FOLK INFLUENCES

Many kinds of music have direct folk influences, and many cellists are expanding their instrument across cultures. Robert Een and Barry Phillips have helped extend the cello into folk styles. Check out Natalie Haas or Abby Newton for Celtic work. Saskia Rao de Haas has studied the classical music of northern India. She plays a unique cello/sitar hybrid.

If you are only familiar with Western music, you can get cello drones on a recoding (looped) to get started. Playing unfamiliar scales/modes along with the drone can help your ears. The cello has three available lower open drone strings that you can simultaneously bow while soloing on the next higher string. For example, you can bow on the D string while improvising on the A as heard on the next audio track.

IMPROVISATION: MAKE IT EASY

You don't have to be able to follow fast chord changes to be able to improvise. Start with one pitch, and find all the ways you can change the tone and make up rhythms with that pitch. Pick two or three pitches, and find where they are in all octaves on the fingerboard. Practicing scales (including the modes) and arpeggios will help you know your way around the cello and aid in fluid improvisation. If you play a note that sounds wrong, slide slowly away from the note to something that sounds better.

Matt Turner, Erik Friedlander, Matt Haimovitz, Wolfram Huschke, Erich Kory, Matthew Brubeck, and Dimos Goudaroulis are some of today's leading improvising cellists.

SPECIAL EFFECTS WITH ACOUSTIC

You do not need an effects processor to make strange sounds on the cello. Explore the different sounds available with **glissando** (sliding the left hand up and down the string), or a harmonic glissando (sliding, but not pressing fingers down). Take techniques you already know and combine them. For example, once you have confident harmonics, combine them with glissando, sul ponticello, pizzicato, etc.

The following audio track demonstrates a normal gliss first, contrasted with a harmonic gliss. Both are on the D string.

NOISE: SCARY SOUNDS

Put your bow in your fist like a cave man. Now drag the bow across the string as slowly as possible. It can sound like a door creaking. Next, try some very high double stops with consecutive, heavy down-bows.

You can also try using something other than your bow on the strings. Pencils are a cheap option; just don't drop one in your cello. More interesting sounds can be made bowing below the bridge, using trem-olo, turning a peg down and up while bowing, plucking behind the nut, etc. If you have a friend who's a film maker, now's your chance to record some scary sounds. They sound great with multiple cello tracks layered together as in this audio track.

60 IN THE STUDIO
(WHERE TO SIT, HOW TO MIC)

If you are recording with an acoustic cello, try to record in a studio that has a sound engineer with experience recording classical music. The cello sounds great on a hardwood floor or in a room that has had acoustical treatment. More than one microphone (and the quality of the mic) is important. Have at least two mics, one above and another toward (but not too close to) the bridge. Before recording, warm up and check if you have proper space to move as you normally do while playing.

If you are recording with the electric cello, tell the recording engineer to treat the instrument like an electric guitar or bass. Since the signal is direct, you don't have to worry about anything except extra batteries and headphones.

Bring a cellist or at least a musician along with you to the studio. This person can sit in the sound room with the recording engineer to give you feedback. When in doubt, record it twice. An extra take is worth the time and investment rather than having to go back in the studio and rerecord. Take the time to hear everything you recorded played back.

See **Tip 92** for info on headphones.

61 SIGHTREADING

Professional and amateur orchestra members often sightread in rehearsals. Or, you may be asked to sightread something on a gig (someone may make a request; you have the sheet music, but you've never played it before).

Don't stop. Concentrate on rhythm. Don't worry about proper fingerings or bowings. Instead, try to get most of the notes and the gist of the piece. Graduates of the "school of faking it" know how to look ahead in the music. Pick a realistic tempo after looking at the most difficult sections. It is better to play the piece slowly but at a steady tempo. And again, don't stop.

If playing in a group, ask ahead of time if you are playing it "as written," which means with all repeats. Check if there is a D.C. al Fine (repeat and go through until the end/Fine). Another type of repeat is D.S. al Fine, which means to go back to the sign and play until the Fine. If you are sightreading a fairly easy piece, put in all the articulations and dynamics.

62 HOW TO FAKE IT

Every musician has gotten lost in the music, but the professionals don't let the audience know. For example, what if your music stand falls over during a wedding recessional? The bridal party is coming toward your string quartet; as the cellist, you need to provide that bass line for Handel's *Water Music* finale. Fortunately, you are a consummate professional, and are aware of your key, form, and chord progression. You could play it safe and stick with the tonic and dominant. The tonic is the name of the key you are in, and the dominant is the fifth degree of the scale being used.

Be aware of the road map of the piece. Is there a key or time change? The recapitulation (return of the beginning theme) is easy to recognize, so mark it in the music.

If rehearsal time is limited (or nonexistent), get the music ahead of time and make necessary markings.

63 READING BASS CLEF IS BASSIC

Cello players first learn to read in bass clef. Once they know bass clef, cellists can read bass, bassoon, or trombone parts, or the left hand of a piano part. The bass clef is also called the F clef, because the two dots in the clef sign are around the note F. To learn the names of the lines on the bass-clef staff, people often use the saying "Good Boys Do Fine Always," which is the bass clef lines from bottom to top (G, B, D, F, A). For the spaces the saying is "All Cars Eat Gas" (Wisconsin version: "All Cows Eat Grass").

Memorize that the top string is the top line (A). The D string is the middle line, and the G string is the bottom line. The C string has two ledger lines, and is the lowest note you will read (except a very rare B♯).

64 TENOR CLEF: HOW TO CHEAT

Advanced cello players need to learn the tenor clef. The tenor clef eliminates the need for additional ledger lines in the high range. The best way to learn tenor clef is to memorize the lines and spaces on the staff. However, it is very rare to play in tenor clef on the G or C strings. To cheat, read a note in tenor clef as if it were bass clef, but play the note one string higher. The problem with cheating is that you are often required to play higher than E on the A string. The first tenor clef note many players learn is G on the A string.

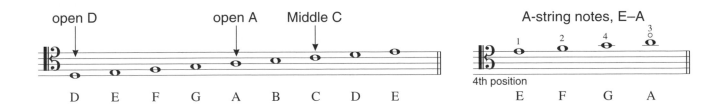

TREBLE CLEF READING

The cello has such a large range that cellists get to learn three clefs! Before you panic, realize that you are beyond intermediate and must already know how music notation works if you are ready for treble clef. Many players already read treble clef from playing piano (the right hand), violin, flute, clarinet, oboe, etc. The treble clef is also called the G clef, because the swirl in the clef sign circles around the note G. Treble clef sayings for the lines and spaces are usually "Every Good Boy Does Fine" for the lines, and the spaces spell FACE (both ascending).

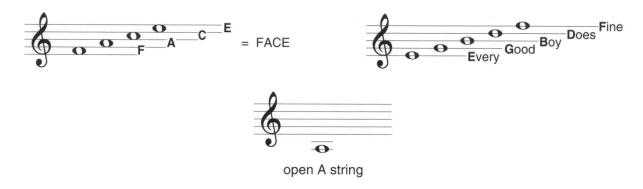

open A string

66 HEAD BANGING
(IT'S NOT JUST FOR METAL)

Since the cellist needs to cue with the face and head (as opposed to the violin and viola scroll), go wild. Make it clear: head up for an up beat, down for a downbeat. We can also use our bow very dramatically, as long as we don't hit anyone.

String players also breathe to indicate cues and phrasing. Unlike wind players, we don't need to breathe to make our instrument speak. However, breathing in (through the nose is fine) as a preparation to start playing together is much more professional than counting off.

To learn more about cues, take a conducting course or read a book about conducting. The best players know what conductors know about communication. Check out *Conducting Technique* by Brock McElheran (Oxford University Press) or *The Modern Conductor* by Elizabeth A.H. Green (Prentice Hall).

Communication in the group

Whether you perform in a classical, jazz, or rock group, communication is very important. Discuss and write in the music who is cueing in a certain section. Make sure everyone can see the drummer if that is who will be cueing a section. Many groups have a regular set up for rehearsal. This can be drastically changed at a performance venue when the headliners are stage hogs who haven't left enough room. Plan your set up ahead of reserving a session in a recording studio. Take the time and plan what cues may need to be changed to help the music go smoothly.

67 ORCHESTRAL REHEARSAL TIPS

If you are in rehearsal, and have a question about a possible misprint in your part, wait until break and ask the conductor if you can check something in their score. Parts often have misprints, but it should be correct(ed) in the score. If you are the "principal" (section leader), part of your job is to communicate any changes with your section. Another responsibility of the principal player is to be aware of the other string sections' bowings, and even the wind players' articulations if you share a line in the music.

Section Tip: If you are a "section" cellist, you are not the principal player. You have to follow that person's bowings. If you have a problem with that, practice and become the principal player for the next season. If you are third or second chair, you may be expected to fill in as the principal if that person misses a concert or rehearsal. Learn all solos ahead of time.

Rehearsal Etiquette

The best players have well-marked parts: always have a pencil. Cellists have the advantage of being able to talk, chew gum, or even eat while playing. Refrain from these behaviors—it irritates the wind players, or worse, the conductor.

68 CHORDS
(TRIPLE AND QUADRUPLE STOPS)

Triple and quadruple stops are almost always played on string instruments from the bottom up. Bow the bottom two notes together and use the rest of the bow (more than half) to play the top two notes immediately after. Use the whole bow with plenty of vibrato. If you are plucking, strum evenly from the bottom note up, like a guitarist or pianist.

The next two examples are taken from "Sonate" by Bréval and feature triple and quadruple stops.

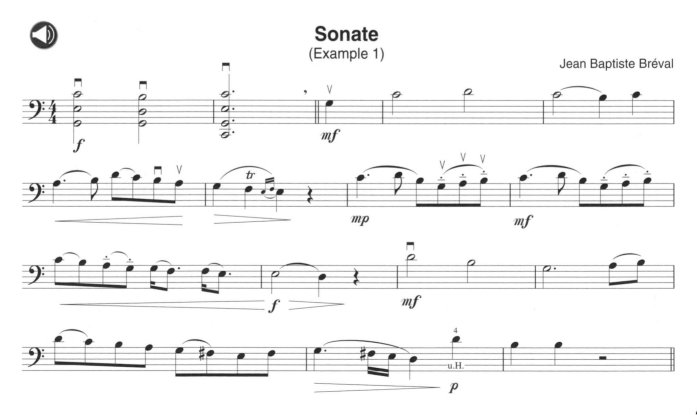

Sonate
(Example 1)

Jean Baptiste Bréval

Sonate
(Example 2)

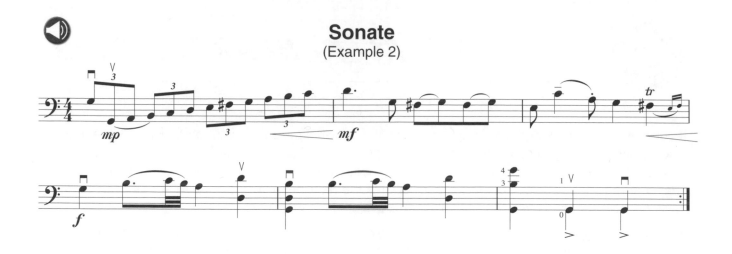

69 THE STANDING CELLIST

Turn down your C string peg until it is at a 40 degree angle from the neck. Now make it stick in the peg box, like when you tune. It may be uncomfortable, but hook your C peg behind your ear, and carefully stand while playing. Before you are ready to walk and play, make sure your part is memorized. Remember that your part may need to be altered if you have notes on the C string (transpose up an octave).

If you would like to just stand and play, you will need a very long endpin and a crate or box under your left foot. Another option is a modified guitar strap. The cello was not designed to be played while standing, so whatever you do, make sure you can play just as well standing as sitting. A standing player is often referred to as a "strolling cellist."

70 CLASSICAL GIG CHECKLIST

Be prepared. Check ahead and find out about the expected dress. Most professional orchestras wear formal black (conservative dressy black for women, men traditionally in tuxedos). Chamber groups and amateur ensembles may wear black and white, or dark dress clothes. A black jacket is handy for both women and men, with pockets to store rosin, cloth, and a rockstop when entering and exiting the stage.

If you play in an orchestra, always have a copy of your music with markings. Never assume that your stand partner will be there. If you missed a rehearsal, show up early the next rehearsal and copy markings you may have missed. Such markings may consist of bowings, fingering suggestions, cuts, repeats, etc.

Don't forget business cards, which should include contact information as well as the variety of events you can do, and the variety of instruments available. Keep a stand light and folding stand in your car.

71 PLAYING AN OUTDOOR GIG

Sunglasses and repellent are necessary. Have a plan for rain included in your contract, indicating that you require shelter. If you have long hair, plan for extremely windy weather. Remember that jacket from **Tip 70**? Have it in your car in case of weather changes.

Music Stands

While a folding stand may be lighter and smaller to carry, a heavy concert stand won't blow over as easily during that wedding ceremony right by the lake. Three-page pieces are no longer an issue if you spring for $12.99 and buy stand extenders.

Clothespins

If you don't have your music memorized, have a bunch of clothespins handy, even for indoor gigs. Gigs have been played in gymnasiums and even churches where the fans blew everyone's music around.

Plexiglass

Have a sheet of Plexiglass to put over your music to keep it in place. A sheet cut to 11" by 17" works well. This may eliminate the need for clothespins and also provides extra weight to help keep the music stand stable. A sheet of plexiglass is heavy enough to keep the music flat.

Extra filler

Be prepared for a wedding ceremony to start late. Other musicians may have car trouble and could be late. If you have an extra fifteen minutes of your own music along to fill the void, you can help the event go smoothly and end up with some solo gigs.

72 CONTRACT IDEAS

Regardless of the event, expect half of your fee in advance, and the rest at the gig after you are done playing. List yourself as "musicians' representative" in the contract. Don't list the other players' names, in case someone needs to get a sub. Send your client two copies of the contract, with instructions to sign both copies and mail one back to you. Retain a gig contract template on your desktop, so all you have to do is plug in the dates and names. Have a rain clause, armless chair requirement, and cancellation scenario. Communicate with your client about repertoire. Let them know that there might be an additional fee if you have to purchase any sheet music. Often times, if the wedding party requests special music, it is their responsibility to purchase the sheet music and give/lend you a copy.

73 MUSIC BINDER

A binder for each style of music (one for classical, one for pops, one with charts from a fake book) with the music in order of the event can help the performance go smoothly. With the music in a three-ring binder, you can change the order easily for the next performance. Be aware that heavy binders do not work well with wimpy wire/folding stands.

74 JAZZ GIG CHECKLIST

Bring your ax and a chair. If just jamming, the checklist is short. If your group has charts to read, you'll need a music stand, stand light, and extension cord. A fake book is good to have along for on-the-spot repertoire decisions and requests. Bass-clef versions are best, such as *The Real Book* volumes 1, 2, and 3, published by Hal Leonard Corporation.

75 ROCK GIG CHECKLIST

Have extra earplugs along, and one of your band mates (or an audience member) will be eternally grateful. Use headphones to warm up backstage, or to plug into your tuner or cello. Don't forget your amp. A change of clothes (or at least a different shirt) could be handy. Check **Tip 76** for your extended list.

76 EXTRA, EXTRA

Bring along patch cords, power strip, duct tape, set list, drum throne (or your own small folding chair—never expect the venue to provide you with a chair that is just right for your playing needs), stand light, extension cord, amp, bow, spare set of used strings, an old bridge, and a folding stand.

Spare Batteries

Always put a new set of batteries into your gig necessities just before sound check for the cello, preamp, flashlight, mic, etc.

Label Maker

Have all of your belongings labeled. If something gets left behind in North Carolina and you live in Wisconsin, you have a much better chance of getting it back, or being able to claim it. Even if your label is made of cheap masking tape, it's better than your item not being labeled and lost forever.

77 BUSINESS TIP

If you want gigs for yourself or your group (who doesn't?), get started on a promotional kit. Include a binder or folder with plenty of business cards, rates, a thumb drive or demo CD (even if they contain just excerpts), a list of available repertoire, and a performance calendar. Reviews and any other press clippings are helpful. You can also include a group photo and the members' bios. All of your promotional information can also be posted on an individual or group website.

Contact your group's members and have a plan for how many gigs will work, and when players are available. Hire the most versatile players and have backup parts, if possible. If your violist is not available, have a violinist on third violin parts.

If you want to play weddings, go to a florist, wedding planner, or chef and propose a business arrangement. It can be merely posting each other's fliers or giving referrals. Many engaged couples will tack up ads in newspapers or on college campus bulletin boards. Some music departments have a list of available players for events.

78 SOUND CHECK

For electric/amplified gigs, be demanding. Be able to tell the sound person how many channels you need, and what your role is in the group (treat the cello like the lead guitar, rhythm guitar, or like a bass). Check the sound effects that you use most often. If your group has a drum set, understand that the drummer will need to check the amplification for each tom, the snare, and bass drum, and cymbals, so bring a book along.

Once each instrument has been checked, the group needs to play together to get the balance levels set. At this time it is beneficial to have someone out in the audience area to listen for balance, especially someone who knows how your group sounds. Most importantly, don't be afraid to communicate to the sound person what you need to hear more and/or less of onstage.

STRETCHING AND WARM-UPS

You are never too young to start stretching before playing. No one wants to end up with tendonitis or surgery. If you are running late to a gig, there are stretches and exercises that you can do in the car. Your playing and endurance will improve if you warm up and stretch before playing, especially in the winter. Stretch your legs, back, shoulders, and neck before and after playing.

Car Stretch

I saw a guitar player do this one while driving! It impressed me, so I practiced it and now I can warm up in the car. Hold your hand up with all fingers pointing up. Bend one finger down at a time, one joint at a time (Fig. 1).

Hand Stretches

Make tight fists for ten seconds, then relax and slowly point your fingers down. Next, extend all fingers out as far as possible and hold for ten seconds. Rest for a few seconds between exercises. You can also give each little joint of every finger a gentle massage.

Rest your hands flat on a table or counter. Slowly raise both hands up as high as possible. After holding for ten seconds, relax.

Curl your fingers over so that the smallest joints are bent into a square shape. Curl the finger "boxes" down into fists, then bend the fists over so the wrists are bent (Figs. 2–4).

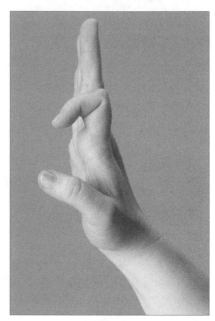

Fig. 1

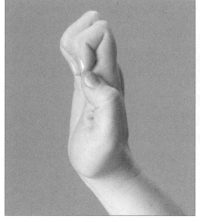

Fig. 2

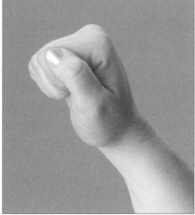

Fig. 3

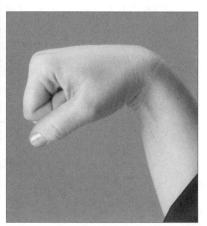

Fig. 4

 # TUNING IN THE ENSEMBLE

In a symphonic orchestra, the ensemble usually tunes to the oboe player's A, which is the same octave as a violin's open A. String orchestras tune to the concert master (first chair of the first violin section). Be aware that when an orchestra tunes onstage, this is merely a check. Players should have already tuned and warmed up back stage.

If you play in a band or nontraditional ensemble, check your open A with the keyboard or piano. Also check your open G string with the bass player. They should match, whether it is acoustic or electric bass. Check your open A, D, and G with a violin or viola player. Their open string should match your octave harmonic. If your group has a guitar player, you can check their G, A, and D strings.

Wind ensembles and concert bands tune to B♭. Be aware that young wind players are used to tuning to B♭. Youth and amateur orchestras often tune the strings first to an A, followed by the winds to a B♭. If there is no oboe (or the oboe player is not reliable), the ensemble can tune to a piano or mallet percussion.

CHECK YOUR BRIDGE AND BODY

Just like getting your car or home ready for winter, get your cello ready as well. Periodically check for warping, cracks, or opening seams as the weather changes. A seam is where two panels meet. A crack on the front panel of your cello is much more urgent than an open seam. Some players use a winter bridge. They often install them before the first frost of the year. Any bridge adjustment or string changes can make the cello out of tune, so try not to have work done close to a performance.

82 HUMIDIFYING

A small sponge in a plastic container with small holes works as well as the commercial humidifier. You should use a humidifier November through March, or at least when there is snow on the ground. Do not over humidify. Make sure the sponge inside is squeezed out so that no dripping can occur. Water damage can be very expensive, and may ruin an instrument's sound. Some humidifiers or instrument cases include a hygrometer, which measures the amount of humidity in the air.

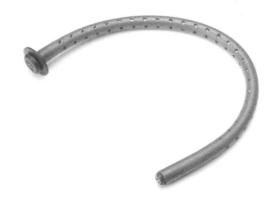

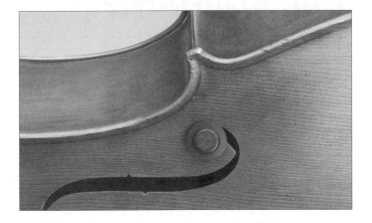

Give your cello time to adjust (ten minutes) if you are bringing it in from the cold or hot weather. It should never sit too long in the car, direct sunlight, or next to a heating and cooling vent. Your cello may also react to extreme changes in humidity.

83 TAKE IT TO THE SHOP

If something is rolling around inside your cello, your sound post has probably fallen over. The bass bar inside the cello can also come loose. Take it to a music store as soon as possible. These are somewhat simple repairs, but you need the proper tools. If you have open seams or a crack in your cello, be aware that whoever repairs it may remove the top panel entirely. Your cello might need to stay in the shop for a couple days.

Unexplained rattle

There is nothing more frustrating than the unexplained rattle or buzz! Check if part of a fine tuner is loose at the top or on the tailpiece. Look for the vibration in the pegs, purfling, seams, or the saddle below the tailpiece. Make a note if the sound only happens in a certain range or on one string. Your endpin may rattle with different floor surfaces. Pickups can also make a buzz or rattle. If you have exhausted all possibilities, take it in.

84 BRIDGE ADJUSTING

Once you are a pro at replacing strings and adjusting your bridge, you might be ready to shave down the bridge a bit with light-grade sandpaper. Make sure you have a cloth between the tailpiece and the cello top. Next, carefully loosen the strings and remove the bridge. Just follow the original bridge shape, and don't sand down past the string notches. Rub the notches with graphite (pencil) before putting the bridge back on. Plan ahead when putting the strings back. Examine the peg box to see which strings will pass below the others, and put those on first.

Safety Tip: You may want protective eyewear and gloves. Do your sanding over a garbage can.

85 PLAYING BY EAR, JAMMING

Even if your favorite song has no cello part, you can learn the melody, bass line, or guitar part. You may have to listen several times to get past the beginning, but have patience. Set small, attainable goals, such as being able to play during the chorus section. Take notes about any changes that happen with drums and bass.

If you need to start simple, begin with short tunes for beginners, such as "Mary Had a Little Lamb." Learn it in different keys, and experiment by flatting the third or fifth pitch of the scale used for the piece. Playing by ear will also help you to improve your intonation.

86 PRACTICING: LESS BUT WELL

The most progress will happen with consistent practice. Fifteen minutes every day is better for retention than an hour once a week. To fix a mistake, you should be able to play it at least five times perfectly, or ten times if you really want it fixed. Recording yourself when practicing can be enlightening, if depressing. Play through a piece without stopping, as if it is a performance. Listen to the recording and circle all mistakes in pencil. Force yourself to fix the circled spots first, and then reward yourself by starting at the beginning. The next time you practice a piece, start in the middle or near the end, working on sections at a time. Always starting at the beginning results in the player knowing the beginning well, but not necessarily the whole piece.

87 IMPROVEMENT
(RECORDING AND VIDEOTAPING YOURSELF)

Nothing is more honest and unforgiving than a videotape or unedited recording of your playing. The video can give you the benefit of seeing your posture, and what needs improvement. The audio recording is excellent, instant feedback about your tone, intonation, rhythm, and tempo. If you are working on intonation in a specific section of a piece, listen to a professional recording of it. You can also record the section on a keyboard followed by your cello and compare the results.

88 JITTERS

The best way to defeat performance anxiety is to perform at every opportunity. Get together often with friends and jam. Perform for parents and grandparents. They may not be objective with their feedback, but that is one more performance under your belt. If you are absolutely petrified at the idea of performing in public, join a large amateur ensemble and start by sitting in the back.

A simple technique many performers use before going on stage is to breathe in and out slowly ten times. Be early to performances so you can take your time unpacking and warming up. Eat a light meal or snack near the performance area about an hour before playing, and keep a small bottle of water onstage. Be aware of sugar, caffeine, and alcohol affecting your body before a performance. If you do make a mistake, don't let it show on your face. Remember that the audience is there to enjoy an interesting performance, not to count your mistakes.

89 METRONOMES

A metronome can be your honest (but annoying) friend who will help you keep a steady tempo. Start by practicing with the metronome at a slow tempo, and gradually speed it up. Make sure the metronome is loud enough that you can hear it to stick with the tempo. Amplify it if necessary. Some well-known metronome brands include Korg, Intelli, and Boss. If your band is going to record with a click track, practice with one.

90 CELLO TONE

Keep four things in mind about your gorgeous cello tone: 1) distance from the bridge, 2) bow speed, 3) amount of bow, and 4) pressure. Most string players are told to use more bow to be louder. This is great advice to the upper string players. If they slow down the bow and use less, they start to scratch. Cellists and bassists can use much less bow (less is more), slow down the bow speed, put the bow closer to the bridge, and still get a big sound. You may need to work at using enough pressure to get the C-string to speak. Instead of just pushing harder, use the heavy arm muscles (wrist not too high). It should help to use the lower, heavier half of the bow. Once you are comfortable with your sound, experiment with bow placement and speed.

91 SHREDDING ON THE CELLO

Shredding is a term often applied to guitar players who perform showy passages at blinding speeds. One way to achieve a certain showiness on the cello is to double, triple, and even quadruple your notes. For example, a melody made up of simple quarter notes can be made more exciting by playing each quarter note as two eighth notes, or as four sixteenths.

The following example shows "Twinkle" in its traditional version, followed by a "quadrupled" version. You may notice that the basic melody and rhythm are the same, but the extra bow strokes on each note add a kind of showy variation.

Twinkle – Traditional

Melody by W. A. Mozart

Twinkle – Quadrupled

If you have shredding chops, use them. String players can double eighth notes and make them sixteenth notes without the left hand working harder. Taking quarter or eighth notes and transforming them into sixteenth notes or the constant tremolo can sound very impressive. However, even though a cellist doesn't need to stop and breathe, your audience might. Use your incredible technique sparingly.

 # 92 *PROPER HEADPHONES A MUST!*

When you get to the studio for the first time to record, don't get stuck with those giant headphones. You may not have enough room on the left side of your head because of the C string peg. Unless you are comfortable playing with your head sideways, or don't need the C string at all, you need a solution.

You can get the half headphones (only on the right side), or bring your own smaller in-ear headphones, with the old Walkman-style headphones on the outside. A lot of violinists wear the regular headphones crooked on their heads so they can hear the instrument as usual with their left ear. Be aware of bleed—most players record with a click track (metronome beating quarter notes) to stay together. The click may bleed from your little headphones out on to one of the mics recording your cello. Whatever headphone setup is best for you, practice with them a few times before recording.

93 *PRACTICING ONE STEP AT A TIME*

Pianists often practice "hands separately." String players tend to neglect practicing with just the bow. Start a practice session with various bow techniques. Include all four strings, and every part of the bow.

The best way to improve your left-hand technique and get creative on the cello is to play without the bow. Lindsay Mac and Stephan Katz are both pioneers in the world of cellists who have plucked their way to success. You can also finger notes with the left hand only as a quiet warm-up.

94 TRANSCRIBING

If you want to improve your ear and notation skills, transcribe a solo or song you enjoy. Start with the basics. Listen to small sections at a time, and find out what pitches are being used. If you play a keyboard instrument, it may help with the notation. You can notate the rhythm and pitches separately, then put them together. Whether you use a computer notation program or scratch it out by hand, the process helps you develop musically.

95 SINGING WHILE PLAYING

If you are determined to sing and play well at the same time, make sure you can do both well separately. It seems obvious, but many players (pianists, drumset players, etc.) need to be reminded to practice certain things hands separately before putting them together. Start with a simple rhythm or chord and strum on and off the beat. The easiest singing parts have a small range and are similar in rhythm to the instrumental part. Ed Willet of the duo Chance is the master of singing while playing cello.

96 LISTENING

Listen to great cellists, the best string players, singers, and guitar heroes. The more diverse your listening is, the better your playing will be of different styles. Although listening to cello players is important, you can learn a lot from listening to great players on any instrument in any style and apply something they do to the cello. Even "classical" musicians in most orchestras are expected to be able to play music from the Baroque, Classical, Romantic, Contemporary, and Post-Modern eras, and possibly Pops as well. Some of the best jazz players have a classical background and training, and vice-versa.

In addition to a listening library, many classical players have excerpt books for auditions. A great way to understand music you are learning is to buy the orchestral score (or check it out from a music library). Listening to the recording while following the score can help your reading and aural skills. Dover scores are often recommended for college music majors.

97 CELLO STORAGE

Put the cello on its side, toward the wall, on its stand, in its case, or upright, leaning in a corner with the bridge facing the corner. The tipsy case needs to go on the floor against a chair or on its side with the bridge facing a wall. If you plan to keep your cello out on a stand, make sure it's a sturdy stand that won't tip. If you have an electric cello like the one pictured in **Tip 46**, a proper stand may be hard to come by. The acoustic cello stand can be used, but it is safe to place it against a wall or backed into a corner to keep from tipping. See **Tip 20** for more on cases.

98 CELLO TRAVEL

If your cello needs to travel by bus or train, make sure it sits in the seat on the window side, like a person. You should sit on the aisle to protect it from falling. If you have to take an airplane, the safest plan is to get a shipping case made for the traveling cellist. They are huge and expensive, but will protect the cello. If your instrument is priceless, investigate the possibility of buying an airline ticket for your cello.

If traveling by car, the safest position is once again riding in the seat like a human (you can even use the seatbelt). If you have a soft case, never put it in the trunk.

99 CELLO RENTAL

Whether or not you plan to travel, have your instrument insured. Make sure you have the serial number written down at home in case of the worst scenario.

If you are practical, you will rent for the first year or so of your cello experience. Just like in **Tip 16**, find out what is included with the rental. Some stores have a rent-to-own policy, so that eventually you will have some collateral. Other places have a lease option, in which a portion of your rental fees goes toward purchase. Most rental instruments are for beginner or intermediate players. If you have rented for a couple years, investigate a step up from what you are currently renting.

Pets and children can be dangerous for any instrument. A maintenance/breakage coverage plan is an excellent idea, even if your monthly payments are a bit higher. The plan may include new strings or repairs at half price.

100 A BIT OF HISTORY

The proper name for the cello is *violoncello*, which translates from Italian to "little big violin." The abbreviation is properly cello, 'cello, or vc. The cello did not have an endpin until the middle of the 19th century—it was held between the player's knees. The bow stick used to curve the opposite direction (away from the hair) until Francois Tourte revised it to today's standard shape. The newer shape gives players much more technical ability and power.

101 SURFING FOR CELLISTS

Check out the following websites for more information about stringed instruments, cellists, sheet music, teachers, etc.:

American String Teachers Association (www.astaweb.com)

American Federation of Violin and Bow Makers (www.afvbm.com)

Internet Cello Society (www.cello.org)

Orchestra audition lists (mywebpages.comcast.net/sduck409/audlists.html)

Strings Magazine (www.stringsmagazine.com)

Cellos, sheet music (www.arcomusic.com)

Rock sheet music for strings (www.monalisasound.com)

Books and recordings for improvisation (www.stringimprov.com)

Stringed instrument maker (www.violoncello.com, www.markedwardsviolins.com)

Stringed instruments and information (www.Stringworks.com, www.Glaesel.com)

Alternative Ensembles with Cellists

www.apocalyptica.com (Known for Metallica covers)

www.beyondthewood.com (World music)

www.crookedstill.com (Bluegrass group)

www.far-corner.com (Chamber rock ensemble)

www.fiddle-sticks.com (Celtic, fiddle, and bluegrass ensemble)

www.heartistrymusic.com (Chance; Cello and vocal duo)

www.monalisasound.com (Hampton String Quartet)

www.murderbydeath.com (Alternative rock)

www.rasputina.com (The Ladies' Cello Society)

www.theroyalgardentrio.com (Jazz ensemble)

www.wyndfallrecords.com (Celtic and folk rock ensemble)

Alternative Cellists

www.cellobop.com (Gideon Freudmann)

www.celloman.com (Eugene Friesen)

www.cellovision.com (Erich Kory)

www.daviddarling.com

www.erikfriedlander.com

www.huschke.de (Wolfram Huschke)

www.improvcellist.com (Matt Turner)

www.lindsaymac.com

www.mattbrubeck.com

www.nataliehaas.com

www.rushadeggleston.com

www.rufusmusic.com (Rufus Cappodocia)

www.spaceagepop.com/katz.htm (Fred Katz)

www.voncello.com (Aaron Minsky)

www.wildcellist.com (Corbin Keep)

www.zoekeating.com